Cecilia McDowall

AVE MARIS STELLA

Commissioned by The Portsmouth Grammar School.

The premiere of *Ave maris stella* was given on Armistice Day 2001 by The Portsmouth Chamber Choir, choirmaster James Henderson, and the London Mozart Players, directed by Nicolae Moldoveanu, at St Thomas's Cathedral, Portsmouth. *Ave maris stella* is recorded on Dutton Epoch CDLX 7146.

Material for string orchestra is available on hire.

COMPOSER'S NOTE

I had already started work on *Ave maris stella* when the events of 9/11 forced me to reconsider my choice of words. Suddenly my original selection of war poetry seemed too disturbing, too provocative and raw, for such a sensitive occasion as Armistice Day. As a result I thought again about the text, wanting to bring something to the work that would have a more personal significance for Portsmouth Grammar School and for the City of Portsmouth with its great naval heritage.

The texts of the piece are taken from the Vesper hymn to the Virgin Mary, *Ave maris stella* (Hail, Star of the sea) and two psalms in the Vulgate: Psalm 106, *Qui descendunt* (They that go down to the sea in ships), and Psalm 26, *Dominus illuminatio mea* (The Lord is my light). This last psalm is associated with the Founder of the school, Dr William Smith, who was at Christ Church, Oxford. *Dominus illuminatio mea*, the Oxford University motto, can be seen in one of the three stained glass panels of the school's Boer War Memorial window in Portsmouth Cathedral, commemorating those who lost their lives. This work bears the dedication *pro pace*, and is inspired by the words of Woodrow Wilson: 'The freedom of the seas is the *sine qua non* of peace, equality and cooperation'.

Duration: 12 minutes

MUSIC DEPARTMENT

OXFORD
UNIVERSITY PRESS

Commissioned by The Portsmouth Grammar School

Ave maris stella

pro pace

'the freedom of the seas is the *sine qua non*
of peace, equality and cooperation.' (Woodrow Wilson)

Ave maris stella antiphon, Psalm 26, and Psalm 106 (Vulgate)

CECILIA McDOWALL

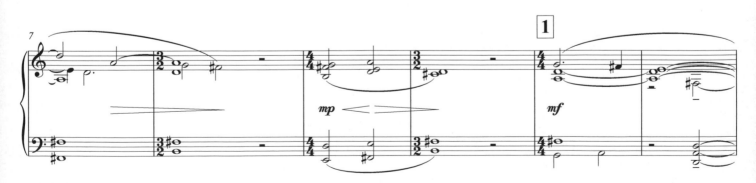

Orchestral material is available on hire from the Publisher's Hire Library, or appropriate agent.

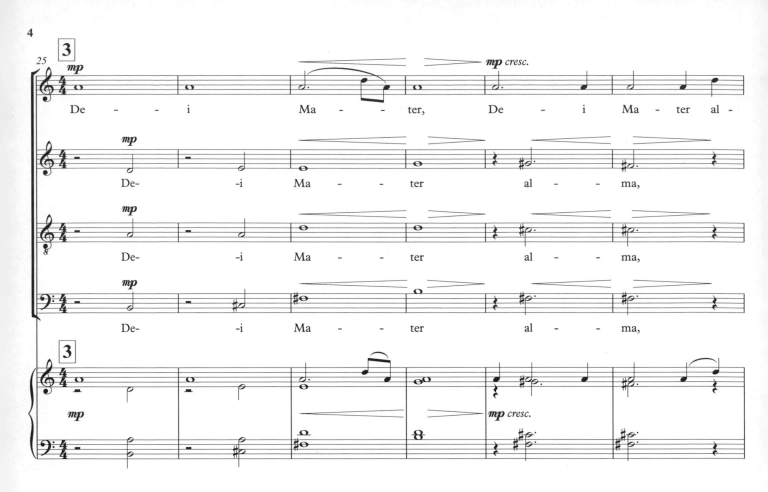

Bo - na cunc - ta pos - ce, bo - na cunc - ta.

Bo - na cunc - ta pos - ce, bo - na cunc - ta.

Bo - na cunc - ta pos - ce, bo - na cunc - ta.

Bo - na cunc - ta pos - ce, bo - na cunc - ta.

10 Expressive and free ♩ = *c.*48 (♩ = ♩)
SOPRANO SOLO *p dolce*

Do-mi-nus il-lu-mi-na-ti-o me - a

pp dolce e sostenuto

et sa-lu-ta-re me - um.___ Do - mi-nus for-ti-tu-do vi-tae me-ae

* Repeat tied A as required.

quem for-mi-da - bo? Do-mi-nus il - lu-mi-na - ti - o me - a.

* The antiphon, *Ave maris stella.*

* Repeat tied A as required.

Processed in England by Enigma Music Production Services, Amersham, Bucks.
Printed in England by Caligraving Ltd, Thetford, Norfolk.